Love of a Lifetime

Caring

Romance

Adoration

Passion

Desire

Happiness

© 2001 Havoc Publishing
San Diego, California
U.S.A.

ISBN 0-7416-1923-7

Text by Kathy Cisneros

www.havocpub.com

Made in Korea

This book is dedicated
to the love shared in the
lives of:

_____

and

_____

You still enchant me

as you did

the first time we met.

The Beginning

Her

The moment I first saw you, you had that look of love in your eyes. Our first encounter took place at: _____

_____

_____

The smallest of details still remain etched forever in my mind about how we met. The date was:_____

_____

_____

I think you were reading my mind with the way we spoke endlessly about: _____

_____

_____

Even today, you still enchant me as you did the first time we met by the way you: _____

_____

_____

Him

You captured my heart so quickly by: _____

_____

If I close my eyes, I can still picture how you were dressed the day we met: _____

_____

_____

I wanted to introduce myself to you as the man of your dreams, but instead, all I could manage to say to you was:

_____

The Dance of Romance

Her

Just the thought of you conjured up so many dreams within me. I imagined the two of us:_____

_____

_____

_____

Every time you were near me I felt: _____

_____

_____

_____

The world was not the same when you weren't around. Whenever you weren't near me, I felt as though: _____

_____

_____

_____

Him

The first time we spoke on the phone, the sound of your voice made me feel: _____

_____

_____

_____

I remember calling
my best friend

and telling her all about you!

You stepped out

of my daydreams

and into my heart.

How It All Began

Her

You stepped out of my daydreams and into my heart on our first date. I'll never forget how we made a date to go to:

_____

_____

_____

I couldn't take my eyes off you when you arrived to pick me up that first time. You were so handsome and I

remember you wearing: _____

_____

_____

It was so easy being with you. That first date, I began to feel as if we had known each other all our lives because:

_____

_____

_____

From there, it was so easy to fall in love with you. We had so many things in common. I was thrilled to learn we

both loved: _____

_____

_____

Place photograph here

Place photograph here

Laugh With Me

Him

I loved how your laughter filled the room when: _____
_____
_____
_____
_____
_____

You always made me smile the way you: _____
_____
_____
_____
_____
_____

The song of our laughter could be heard so distinctly whenever we: _____
_____
_____
_____

I love how
your laughter
fills the room.

*I*n your eyes
You said,
Come find me.
You invited me
So softly
To love.
I responded
To signals
My heart
Was sent,
As I went
Into worlds
You dreamed of.

Family Ties

Her

I couldn't wait to tell everyone about you! The first person I called was: _____

_____

Everyone remarked about how happy I have been since you came into my life. I remember my family saying: _____

_____

_____

Him

When you first met my family, they adored you. Afterwards, they told me I had finally found someone who: _____

_____

_____

_____

I was nervous to meet your family for the first time. They welcomed me and made me feel comfortable by: _____

_____

_____

I saw the family resemblance the first time I met: _____ You even had the same: _____

_____

_____

I laughed when I heard all the stories about you growing up. I even remember being told about the time when you:

_____

_____

_____

How to Love You

Her

I knew it before you ever said a word. Yet you made it all the more special when you told me for the first time you

loved me by: _____

_____

_____

_____

The date is etched in my mind forever as: _____

_____

_____

Him

I wanted to learn everything I needed to know to love you completely.   I wanted to be the one who: _____

_____

_____

_____

_____

I listened carefully to your dreams and aspirations. I wanted to help you reach them by: _____

_____

_____

I will

always love you

with all my heart.

*I wanted
the gift of
magical surprises
to last forever.*

Secrets and Treasures

Her

I knew you trusted me completely when you told me: _____

_____

_____

You knew I trusted you completely, when I opened my heart and told you: _____

_____

_____

Sometimes we said it without a word. There was a bond between us built on the faith we had in one another. It was

perfectly natural for us to just: _____

_____

_____

_____

Him

You treated me to your "spur of the moment" side the time you: _____

_____

_____

_____

You touched me forever when out of the blue you: _____

_____

_____

_____

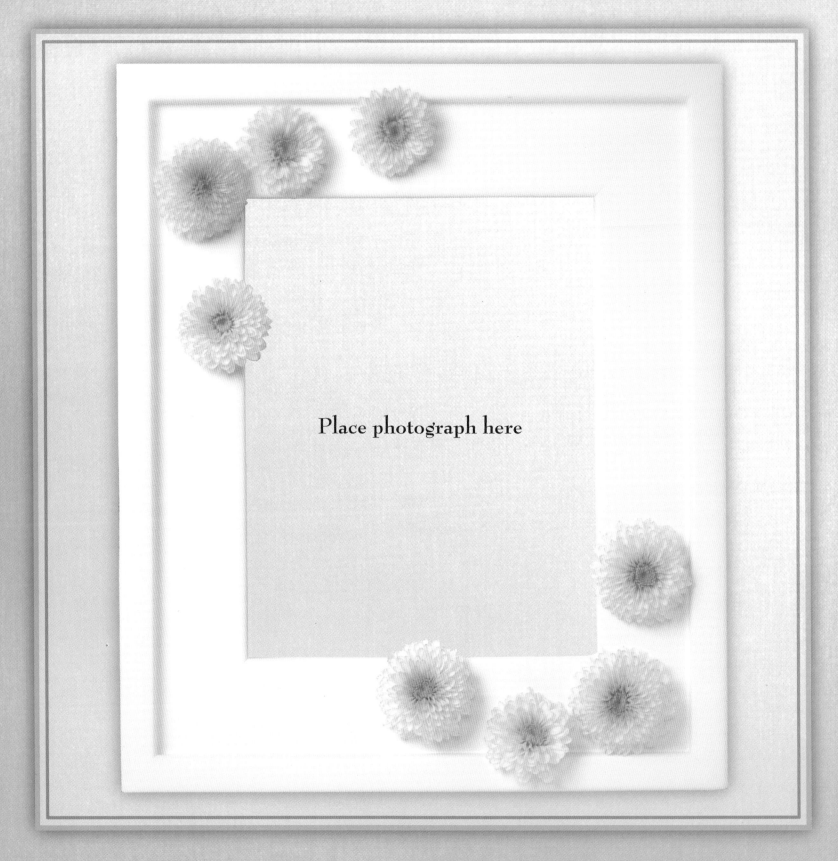

Place photograph here

Place photograph here

Treats and Sweets

Her

I love to surprise you every once in awhile with your favorite snack. Your eyes light up whenever I give you:

_____

_____

You made Valentine's Day so memorable and romantic by feeding me: _____

_____

We indulge in our favorite desserts from time to time on special occasions. You know I can't resist: _____

_____

You have a passion for: _____

_____

Him

We love to spend quiet evenings at our favorite restaurant called: _____

We love it there because: _____

_____

_____

I wondered if you knew how nervous I was planning the first meal I cooked for you. I was relieved at your

reaction when you said: _____

_____

You worked so hard the first time you prepared a meal for us. I noticed the little things you paid so much

attention to. For example: _____

_____

We love to spend quiet evenings

at our favorite restaurant.

Desires

You brought my heart

Desires

I had never felt before

With passion wrapped

In fires

That my soul

Could not ignore.

$\mathcal{Y}$ou brought my heart

Dimensions

With intentions

Deep and true

I was in love

The moment

I found you.

Ask me to listen to stories

you need me to hear.

The Gifts of Each Other

Her

No one person can be everything to another, and yet I longed to be that person for you. If it were possible: _____

_____

_____

_____

_____

Him

Ask me to hold you just for the sake of being held. Holding you to my heart allows me to give you: _____

_____

_____

_____

_____

Ask me to see the world through your eyes and paint me your pictures. Sharing the visions you see brings me:

_____

_____

_____

_____

Nicknames

Her

You made me feel so cherished each time you called me: _____

because I felt: _____

_____

_____

_____

_____

I knew how much it tickled you when I would snuggle up against you and call you my: _____

_____

_____

Him

You would blush so easily each time I called you my: _____

_____

_____

_____

_____

I selected that name for you because: _____

_____

_____

You always make me feel

so special.

Surrender

I let myself surrender
To the wonder
Of your eyes,
I relished every moment
As love took me
By surprise.

I let it take me over
As my soul
Began to soar,
And now I know
I'll love you
In my heart
Forevermore.

The best part

of our arguments

is the way we make up!

Kiss and Make Up!

Her

Together we faced disappointments. It was so hard on both of us when: _____

_____

United we found our greatest strength as a couple, like the time we faced: _____

_____

We have learned not to walk alone and away from each other in difficult times. We were always able to find

solutions together by: _____

_____

_____

Him

It's hard not to laugh about it now, but the first time we argued it was about: _____

_____

_____

You can tell when I'm angry by the way I: _____

_____

_____

I know when you've had just about enough when you say: _____

_____

I love it when we come to an understanding by: _____

_____

_____

Place photograph here

Place photograph here

Precious Treasures

Her

The first bouquet of flowers you ever sent me was: _____

You sent them because: _____

_____

The first time I went shopping for a gift for you, I ended up buying: _____

because: _____

_____

The gift you gave me that I relish the most is: _____

because: _____

_____

Him

The sweetest gift you ever gave me didn't cost a cent. It was the gift of: _____

_____

_____

The first piece of jewelry I surprised you with was: _____

it touched your heart because I remembered: _____

_____

I spent hours choosing your first present. I finally found: _____

_____

_____

I chose it because: _____

_____

I spent hours choosing your first present.

We support

each other's goals.

Careers that Define Us

Her

From an early age, I always knew I wanted to be a: _____

because: _____

_____

_____

With your intelligence and talent, it didn't surprise me to find out you excelled at being a: _____

_____

_____

We supported each other's goals by understanding the sacrifices we would make to achieve them. You said all the

right words when I explained to you my feelings about: _____

_____

_____

Him

People who know me said I always had a natural talent for: _____

My career allows me to develop that talent by: _____

_____

Even though I make a living by being a: _____

I will always harbor a secret dream of becoming a: _____

_____

I will always be grateful that you understood my need to enjoy my career and yet you also encouraged me to pursue:

_____

_____

Meant to be

Who is this new person

That you've touched

Inside of me?

*I*t's as though

You saw in me,

What others

Could not see.

It's as though

This love of ours

Was always

Meant to be.

Matters of the Heart

Her

I will always need to hear you say: _____

_____

_____

_____

_____

Say you love me with more than your words by: _____

_____

_____

_____

_____

_____

_____

_____

I wonder if you know what it does to my heart to hear you say: _____

_____

_____

_____

_____

I don't know if you realize how hard I cried when you told me: _____

_____

_____

_____

Say you love me

with more than your words.

Ecstasy

I'd press my lips

Against yours

And fall in your embrace

Whisper softly

In your ear

With love upon

My face.

$\mathcal{F}$all into surrender

Of the ecstasy

Of you.

And stay forever

So in love,

So much in love

With you.

I would love to see the world

from your eyes.

Send the World Away

Her

It has always been my dream to someday travel to: _____

I want to go there because: _____

_____

_____

_____

You once told me that if you could you would pack your bags for: _____

You said it means so much to you because: _____

_____

I would love to see the world from your eyes if we were ever able to go to: _____

I know it would mean so much to you because: _____

_____

_____

Him

The first place we traveled together was: _____

The most exciting vacation we took was when we traveled to: _____

We had so much fun there because: _____

_____

_____

The most creative fantasy we shared was when we threw caution to the wind and: _____

_____

Music

Her

Our song will always be: _____

by: _____

_____

It was meant for us because: _____

_____

_____

The first song we ever danced to was: _____

by: _____

_____

_____

_____

I remember it clearly because we were: _____

_____

_____

_____

We may vary in our musical tastes but we both love: _____

because: _____

_____

Your laughter

is music

to my soul.

Softly

When you touch me softly,

You lift me to the stars

You give me everything you are

Within this love of ours.

$\mathcal{Y}$ou show me

different sides of you

The world will never see

When you touch me softly,

You touch the heart in me.

We make

a great team!

Fun Together

Him

We would make a great team at: _____

No matter how many times I've tried to explain the sport of _____, you'll never catch on!

I remember a time that you taught me about this sport: _____

_____

_____

_____

Her

It surprised you to learn how much I love the sport: _____

You laughed when you found out and said: _____

_____

_____

You have a passion for: _____

I remember you once talked me into trying: _____

_____

_____

Our favorite activity that challenges us to compete against each other is: _____

_____

You always think that you'll win because: _____

_____

Stay in Love With Me

Her

Never change the way you: _____

_____

_____

_____

Remind me what you love most about me so I never lose that. I want to always be the one who: _____

_____

_____

Him

I adore sense of style. I love to see you dressed up in: _____

_____

_____

I love the scent of your hair and the way you wear it. You are so attractive when you: _____

_____

_____

Your favorite fragrance: _____

It defines you because: _____

_____

_____

_____

I can always tell

when you

walk into a room.

Place photograph here

Place photograph here

Each celebration
was made more special with

you being there.

Celebrations

Her

Do you remember the first holiday we spent together? I will never forget it because: _____

_____

I'll never forget the way we celebrated: _____

_____

During the season of _____ I love being with you and sharing: _____

Remember the time we: _____

_____

Him

You made my birthday very special by: _____

_____

_____

I will never forget when you gave me: _____

I will treasure it always because... _____

_____

My love for you was shown by my gift of... _____

_____

Place photograph here

Place photograph here

Ever After

Her

Let's always promise to: _____

_____

_____

Let's build new memories to cherish as we grow together forever, young at heart. We'll always remain that way by:

_____

_____

_____

Your love has changed my life forever by: _____

_____

_____

_____

Him

Spend the rest of your sunsets with me. Let me see them through your eyes by sharing your:_____

_____

_____

_____

_____

Give me a lifetime to love you.   I will fall in love with you forever because: _____

_____

Wake with me

each sunrise

from now on,

forever.

$\mathcal{Y}$ou are the Love
of my Lifetime,
The one I have dreamed
of so long.
You are the Love
of my Lifetime.
And here in my arms you belong.
You are the one that I treasure.
You are the one I adore.
You are the Love of my Lifetime
And will be forevermore.